ABIDE

Learning to Walk in Intimacy with God

ABIDE

Learning to Walk in Intimacy with God

Learner Guide

Abide: Learning to Walk in Intimacy with God (Learner Guide)
Copyright © 2024 by First Baptist Church Peachtree City in cooperation with Five Mark Ministries

All rights reserved solely by the author. The author guarantees all contents are original and do not infringe upon the legal rights of any other person or work. No portion of this book may be reproduced in any form without written permission from the publisher or author, except as permitted by U.S. copyright law.

This publication is designed to provide accurate and authoritative information in regard to the subject matter covered. It is sold with the understanding that neither the author nor the publisher is engaged in rendering legal, investment, accounting or other professional services. While the publisher and author have used their best efforts in preparing this book, they make no representations or warranties with respect to the accuracy or completeness of the contents of this book and specifically disclaim any implied warranties of merchantability or fitness for a particular purpose. No warranty may be created or extended by sales representatives or written sales materials. The advice and strategies contained herein may not be suitable for your situation. You should consult with a professional when appropriate. Neither the publisher nor the author shall be liable for any loss of profit or any other commercial damages, including but not limited to special, incidental, consequential, personal, or other damages.

The ESV Global Study Bible®, ESV® Bible
Copyright © 2012 by Crossway.

All rights reserved.

The Holy Bible, English Standard Version® (ESV®)
© 2001 by Crossway,
a publishing ministry of Good News Publishers.
All rights reserved.
ESV Text Edition: 2016

Book Cover by Tonya Allen
Contributors: Dr. Craig Hamlin, Dr. Joey Rodgers and Steve Rasmussen

ISBN: 9798871360965
Imprint: Independently published

*I am the Vine; you are the branches. If you **abide** in me and I in you, you will bear much fruit; apart from me, you can do nothing.*
John 15:5

TABLE OF CONTENTS

HOW TO USE THIS LEARNER'S GUIDE .... - 1 -

INTRODUCTION .... - 3 -

THE TRUE VINE .... - 5 -

FEARFULLY AND WONDERFULLY MADE .... - 13 -

A LIVING SACRIFICE .... - 23 -

ABIDE IN THE WORD .... - 31 -

LIVING A SPIRIT-EMPOWERED LIFE .... - 37 -

TRUST APPLIED .... - 45 -

READY TO TELL .... - 53 -

THE SPIRITUAL HOUSEHOLD OF GOD .... - 61 -

LOVING BEYOND LIMITS .... - 69 -

HIDING GOD'S WORD .... - 77 -

FAST FACTS ABOUT FASTING .... - 83 -

MAKING DISCIPLES .... - 91 -

RESOURCES CITED

HOW TO USE THIS LEARNER GUIDE

The Learner Guide for *Abide* is designed to maximize your study of the *Abide* curriculum. There are specific elements for you to engage interactively on a personal level, as well as, with your small group. This Learner's Guide is set up with some featured components:

Connecting to the Story – this helps you with some introductory questions to get you thinking about the story and its application.

Diving into the Story – this helps you learn what the story is about with the outline and Scripture passages.

Diving Deeper – these are questions to give you a major takeaway and practical next steps as you think through what you have learned.

Use the space provided with questions to write down your thoughts. At the end of each chapter, there are **GROW** Scriptures. These Scriptures correspond to the **GROW** workbooks on which *Abide* is based. An additional resource is the **GROW** books that are designed to be used with a smaller group of men and women in an organic bible-study, life-to-life setting.

For more information on how to purchase **GROW** materials, visit www.joeyrodgers.com.

INTRODUCTION

I am the Vine; you are the branches. If you remain in me and I in you, you will bear much fruit; apart from me, you can do nothing.

John 15:5

In John 15, somewhere between the upper room and the garden of Gethsemane, Jesus shared with his disciples is supposed to essential lesson on followship – the lesson of abiding. To abide in Christ is to remain in him. It is to live in alignment under is influence and authority. It is to be grafted into intimacy salvation so that the source of our lives is the Holy Spirit.

Often in the Gospels, Jesus used familiar analogies to illustrate important lessons. Just as a branch depends entirely on the vine for life, growth, and sustenance so that it might bear fruit, so too must every Jesus-follower depend completely on the Lord for their provision as well.

The heart of abiding is maintaining unbroken communion with God. It is to be in a constant state of connection. Imagine an apple tree. While the tree is full of apples hanging from its branches, at the base of the tree is a single branch that has been severed from the trunk. Will that branch ever again be able to produce apples? Of course not! Why? Because it is no longer connected to the trunk and able to receive life, growth, and sustenance from the tree. Life is in the tree – and the only way the branch can have life is to be connected to the tree. The same is true regarding our relationship with God.

Life with the Father begins at salvation. As the Apostle Paul explains in Romans 11, upon salvation, believers are grafted into a relationship with God. The Holy Spirit is deposited into our lives and if we will walk in continual submission and surrender, then we will begin to walk with God in intimacy with the purpose of knowing him and living to honor him. The result of such intimacy is that our lives will supernaturally begin to bear fruit. As God lives in us and through us, our lives will produce the fruit of the Spirit and the fruit of the Great Commission.

Over the next twelve weeks, we want to invite you to join us on a journey to abide in Christ. From the pulpit to our daily walk, we are going to invest time in learning how to walk intimately with God through the application of the spiritual disciplines God has made available to us. We look forward to growing with you in Christ.

Solo de gloria!

Session 1
The True Vine

John 15:1-11

Connections are essential to the human experience. Connections help people flourish as they develop friendships, relationships, and selfless love. Without connections to people, we lose the purpose for why God created us within a human race. Herman Melville wrote, "We cannot live only for ourselves. A thousand fibers connect us with our fellow men; and among those fibers, as sympathetic threads, our actions run as causes, and they come back to us as effects." If connecting with people is essential for human flourishing, then connecting with God must be of paramount importance. God created us for relationship, and our lives are not fulfilled until we can rest in his abiding presence and power. Our connection with God begins at the moment of faith in him and continues growing as a plant's shoot bursts forth from the ground to bear fruit, useful to all who need it. Without an abiding, intimate walk with Jesus Christ, we cannot fully enjoy the life God created us to have or bear the fruit God created us to bear for the benefit of others. Our lives grow inward when we are disconnected from Christ, but when we abide in him, he produces through us a beautiful life of love, joy, peace, patience, kindness, goodness, faithfulness, gentleness and self-control.

Jesus is the Connection to a life of utter fruitfulness; a life that matters into eternity. He is the Vine that connects you to meaning in life. Therefore, see the work of the True Vine, know the expectations of the True Vine, learn the promises of the True Vine and enjoy the fruit of the True Vine.

👣 Connecting to the Story

What is it about being independent that appeals to everyone? How can our hunger for independence be a detriment in our relationship with God?

👣 Diving into the Story

What's It All About
Jesus uses his last few earthly days with his disciples to teach them how to glorify God. The disciple's life is all about glorifying God, and God is glorified when his disciples bear much fruit (John 15:8). The process of bearing fruit happens through an abiding relationship with the true vine, Jesus Christ. Jesus clearly states in John 15:1, "I am the true vine." This unequivocal statement of Jesus' identity is among six other statements Jesus makes of himself. But also, Jesus mentions the Father as the vinedresser. The job of the vinedresser is to care for the vine by caring for the branches. The Father lifts up the branches that are not producing and cleans them before placing them back up on the trellis. For those branches producing fruit, he prunes so they can bear more fruit. The branches are Jesus' disciples. Their only role is to bear fruit. They do not have the power to produce fruit, but as they remain connected to the vine and experience the nutrients the vine supplies, they bear more and more fruit. If a branch is disconnected from the vine, the branch has no life source and withers. Withered vines are no good because vines cannot be used for building anything. Their only purpose at that point is to be burned.

Jesus' analogy is straightforward. If a disciple remains connected to Jesus, the natural flow of life in Christ will flow into the life of the disciple. The life of Jesus will be clearly seen and experienced by others when there is closeness to Christ. This closeness produces the fruit of answered prayer, increased faith and the character of Christ in the disciple. There is no greater purpose in the disciple's life than bearing fruit. It demonstrates dependency on Jesus and through dependency on Jesus, the Lord is glorified. The more I need Jesus, the more others see how much Jesus can do for us and through us.

The Big Idea

God is most glorified in his disciples and produces much fruit in their lives when they remain in an indwelling and abiding relationship with Jesus Christ. The disciple's life is powerless and fruitless without this abiding intimacy with Christ.

Christ in the Text

Jesus Christ is the True Vine that produces a fruitful, meaningful life in every disciple who remains in him, and without him, disciples of Jesus can do nothing that truly lasts.

#1 The Work of the True Vine

I am the True Vine, and my Father is the Vinedresser. Every branch in me that does not bear fruit he takes away, and every branch that does bear fruit he prunes, that it may bear more fruit. Already you are clean because of the word that I have spoken to you.

John 15:1-3

1. Why is it important to prune a vine?

2. What is God doing in the Christian's life when he brings trials or discipline into their life?

3. What are some ways you have seen or "felt" God pruning you recently?

2 The Expectation of the True Vine

Abide in me, and I in you. As the branch cannot bear fruit by itself, unless it abides in the vine, neither can you, unless you abide in me. I am the vine; you are the branches. Whoever abides in me and I in him, he it is that bears much fruit, for apart from me you can do nothing. If anyone does not abide in me he is thrown away like a branch and withers; and the branches are gathered,
thrown into the fire, and burned.

John 15:4-6

1. Jesus clearly states the position of his disciples and himself as the branch and vine. What are the implications of living independently as a branch from the vine? How does this relate to daily life?

2. What does life look like disconnected from Christ versus one dependent on a daily, intimate connection? What are the practical outcomes?

#3 The Promise of the True Vine

If you abide in me, and my words abide in you, ask whatever you wish, and it will be done for you. By this my Father is glorified, that you bear much fruit and so prove to be my disciples.

John 15:7-8

1. What does Jesus mean when he says, "Ask whatever you wish, and it will be done for you"? Is this a blank check from God?

2. How does abiding in him change or inform the way we pray?

3. What does bearing much fruit have to do with asking whatever we wish?

#4 The Fruit of the Vine

As the Father has loved me, so have I loved you. Abide in my love. If you keep my commandments, you will abide in my love, just as I have kept my Father's commandments and abide in his love. These things I have spoken to you, that my joy may be in you, and that your joy may be full.

John 15:9-11

1. What does it look like to abide in your love for your spouse or friend?

2. What does Jesus say is the key to abiding in his love? How and why would you apply this principle?

3. How can abiding in Christ and obeying his commandments bring fullness of joy to our life?

Diving Deeper

1. What is the biggest takeaway from this passage?

2. What are some ways you could apply this passage?

   Is there a sin to avoid?
   Is there a promise to claim?
   Is there a command to obey?
   Is there an example to follow?
   Is there praise to give?

3. Why did Jesus make such a big deal about abiding and fruitfulness?

4. What will you apply specifically this week?

5. Who will hold you accountable this week for your response to Question 4?

In his book, *Abiding in Christ: Becoming Like Christ Through an Abiding Relationship with Him*, Paul Chappell writes, "In the old western days, a man was walking down the road carrying a bag of grain on his shoulder. Another man was riding along the road in a buckboard pulled by a horse. He came up beside the man carrying the grain and said, "Jump up here on the buckboard with me. It's too hot to be walking today." The man said, "Thank you," and got up onto the seat with his grain still on his shoulder. After a while, the driver said, "Why don't you put that grain down and relax?" The passenger said, "Oh, no. It's enough that you would allow me to ride—I would never ask you to carry my load, too!" This is what many Christians do. They say, "Lord, I know You can save me, forgive my sins, and give me a home in Heaven, but I wouldn't ask You to carry my load too!" Friend, He said, "I want to abide with you. I want to carry your load and be your life."

GROW Passages for Week 1

1. John 15:1-13

2. Colossians 1:9-14

3. 1 Timothy 4:7-8

4. Hebrews 12:1-3

5. Colossians 3:1-17

Session 2

Fearfully and Wonderfully Made

Psalm 139

To be known! Everyone wants someone to know them, to know their name, to care about their wellbeing and to feel as if they mattered in the world. When Henry Norris Russell, the Princeton astronomer, had concluded a lecture on the Milky Way, a woman came to him and asked, "If our world is so little, and the universe is so great, can we believe God really pays any attention to us?" Dr. Russell replied, "That depends, madam, entirely on how big a God you believe in." God is beyond all comprehension. His presence cannot be contained and his knowledge never apprehended. God is limitless and boundless. And yet, he knows every single one who has ever lived and will ever live in an instant. God does not need a moment to recall a name, but instantly knows because he has always known. The Lord has created each person intricately with DNA, flesh and bones. Every person's fingerprint tells a different story unique to them, and yet, they all fall under the image of God.

To know that the God of all creation, the only true and holy God, knows your name and cares about your life is extraordinary. Paddick Van Zyl writes, "Think about this for a moment – God who created all things and sustains all things, knows perfectly well about your circumstances and storms which you may find yourself in right at this moment in time. He has not forgotten you or about you. He knows your name. He created your eyes and your personality. He knows you far better than you know yourself."

You are fearfully and wonderfully made. That fact alone should cause you to worship and praise the One who gave you life. That life deserves your utmost of love and devotion because it was purchased with the blood of Jesus Christ. Therefore, live confidently knowing that God knows everything and is with you always, working around you and for you, and dealing justly with those who would do evil.

Connecting to the Story

What is the danger in following someone whom you do not know or trust? What are some wrong ideas about God that can impact how we view ourselves?

Diving into the Story

What It's All About
Psalm 139 sets out to definitively show us that we are not God. He is beyond all and above all. And yet, he cares for each person intimately and provides his presence, power, and protection throughout life. In his book, How to Stay Christian in College, J. Budziszewski writes, "God is utterly other than us – other in a way we express with the word holiness. Yes, He dwells within each Christian, but He's not you. He isn't the same as you, He isn't a part of you, and He isn't a 'higher' you. Yes, you're made in His image, but you're not Him. You're not the same as Him, you're not part of Him, and you aren't a 'splinter' of Him – nor will you ever be. He doesn't depend on anything else because He is what everything else depends on. He can't be explained

by anything else because He is what everything else must be explained by. Although we can know what He has taught us about Himself, we can never comprehend Him completely because He is greater than our minds. Anything He wills, He can do. He not only upholds supreme power but He also uses it. Nothing can defeat Him and nothing can happen contrary to His will. He is also supremely good-light with no darkness. Although evil is real, He detests it and brings it to judgment. He knows everything, He pays attention to everything, and nothing escapes His notice. He's not just a What and a Who, like me or like you, but one What in three Whos – one God in three Persons: Father, Son, and Holy Spirit. There is no one like Him. He is set apart. He is what He is, and there was never a time when He was not."[i]

If we are going to have a clear picture of ourselves, who we really are, and what we really need in life and eternity, we must have a clear view of God. To have a wrong view of God is to have a wrong view of ourselves. In a time when people have replaced God with science or their intellectual prowess, humanity has become bent inwardly toward themselves. St. Augustine used the Latin phrase, "incurvatus in se", to be curved inward as a way to describe the human tendency for self-absorption. The Protestant Reformer, Martin Luther followed up on Augustine's premise by saying, "Our nature, by the corruption of the first sin, [being] so deeply curved in on itself that it not only bends the best gifts of God towards itself and enjoys them or rather even uses God himself in order to attain these gifts, but it also fails to realize that it so wickedly, curvedly, and viciously seeks all things, even God, for its own sake."[ii]

The writer of Psalm 139, King David, knew that he had a desperate desire to truly know God. He invited God into every corner and crevice of his life. David wanted to know God and be known by God. He called out to God to "search me, O God, and know my heart!" That is the cry of every person who has placed their faith in Jesus Christ. We have given up our independence for a life of dependence on our

Creator. David wanted to live every moment of his life pleasing the Lord. He wanted God to be in his thoughts, and he wanted his thoughts to be directed by God. David's life would be one of total surrender. And yet, through the selfishness of his sin with Bathsheba and the subsequent cover-up attempt with Uriah that led to his murder, David found in God a source of power and presence that he needed to help him recover from a major moral failure. Because David had a right view of God, he could see himself correctly, and by it, know that he could trust God and must trust God above himself. He is all we need!

The Big Idea
God, who knows all things intimately and completely, is praised as Creator, Sustainer, and Judge of both the wicked and the righteous.

Christ in the Text
Jesus Christ knows you intimately and completely in a redemptive relationship of love designed to compel your heart to desire him above all things.

#1 God Knows

O Lord, you have searched me and known me! You know when I sit down and when I rise up; you discern my thoughts from afar. You search out my path and my lying down and are acquainted with all my ways. Even before a word is on my tongue, behold, O Lord, you know it altogether. You hem me in, behind and before, and lay your hand upon me. Such knowledge is too wonderful for me;
it is high; I cannot attain it.

Psalm 139:1-6

1. In a time when people want their privacy, why should we not want God to know everything about us?

2. Do you find the omniscience of God bothersome or comforting? Why?

3. Why would this passage not set well with those who do not believe in God?

#2 God is There

Where shall I go from your spirit? Or where shall I flee from your presence? If I ascend to heaven, you were there! If I make my bed in Sheol, you are there! If I take the wings of the morning and dwell in the uttermost parts of the sea, even dare your hand shall lead me, and your right hand shall hold me. If I say, "Surely the darkness shall cover me, and the light about me be night," even the darkness is not dark to you; the night is bright as the day, for darkness is as light with you.
Psalm 139:7-12

1. How is God's omnipresence (God is everywhere) different from the teaching of pantheism (God is in everything)?

2. How does God's omnipresence impact the way you handle life's difficult situations?

3. Why would you ever not want to be in the presence of God?

#3 God Works

For you formed my inward parts; you knitted me together in my mother's womb. I praise you, for I am fearfully and wonderfully made. Wonderful are your works; my soul knows it very well. My frame was not hidden from you, when I was being made in secret, intricately woven in the depths of the earth. Your eyes saw my unformed substance; in your book were written, every one of them, the days that were formed for me, when as yet there was none of them. How precious to me are your thoughts, O God! How fast is the sum of them! If I would count them, they are more than the sand. I awake, and I am still with you.

Psalm 139:13-18

1. Describe your comfort knowing God intimately and intentionally fashioned you before you were born.

2. How does this reality impact the way you live out your faith, view life and view others?

#4 God Deals Justly

Oh that you would slay the wicked, O God! O men of blood, depart from me! They speak against you with malicious intent; your enemies take your name in vain. Do I not hate those who hate you, O Lord? And do I not loathe those who rise up against you? I hate them with complete hatred; I count them my enemies. Search me, O God, and know my heart! Try me and know my thoughts! And see if there be any grievous way in me, and lead me in the way everlasting!

Psalm 139:19-24

1. Why should Christians be jealous for the name of the Lord?

2. What are some appropriate responses toward those who openly and aggressively reject the Lord and dishonor his name?

3. Why should Christians make it a regular discipline to ask God to do an inventory of their heart?

👣 Diving Deeper

1. What is the biggest takeaway from this passage?

2. What are some ways you could apply this passage?

   Is there a sin to avoid?
   Is there a promise to claim?
   Is there a command to obey?
   Is there an example to follow?
   Is there praise to give?

3. What does God's omnipotence, omnipresence, and omniscience speak into your life as you think about the daily challenges you face?

4. What will you apply specifically this week?

5. Who will hold you accountable this week to your response to Question 4?

"There is no event so commonplace but that God is present within it, always hiddenly, always leaving you room to recognize him or not...because in the last analysis all moments are key moments, and life itself is grace."
~ Friedrich Buechner

GROW Passages for Week 2

1. Mark 1:35; Luke 5:15-16

2. Psalm 91:1-16

3. Psalm 139:1-25

4. Isaiah 40:28-31

5. Matthew 6:5-7

Session 3
A Living Sacrifice

Romans 12:1-2

Each Sunday, church goers drive their cars to a local church gathering in a building, school or home and gather to sing, give their offerings, serve and hear a message. Then they leave, and for the most part, they go about their routine lives through the week earning a living. On the weekends, they play sports, work on the house or plan some activity. Then, on Sunday, they get up drive their cars to a local church gathering in a building, school or home and gather to sing, give their offerings, serve and hear a message. Then…Yes, it's the routine of ordinary Christian life. There could be a service project mixed in here or there, but mostly, it's the routine. Is this what the Christian life is supposed to look like? Is this all Jesus had in mind for his disciples when he died on the cross? The routine might be unavoidable, but sacrifices in our lives must cause our faith to rise above the practice of church gathering to a heart of worship, leading to profound holiness and commitment to Christ.

In the mid-seventeenth century, a somewhat well-known Englishman was captured by Algerian pirates and made a slave. While a slave, he founded a church. When his brother arranged his release, he refused freedom, having vowed to remain a slave until he died in order to continue serving the church he had founded. Today a plaque in an Algerian church bears his name. David Livingstone, the renowned and noble missionary to Africa, wrote in his journal, "People talk of the sacrifice I have made in spending so much of my life in Africa. Can that be called sacrifice which is simply paid back as a small part of the great debt owing to our God, which we can never repay? Is that a sacrifice which brings its own reward of healthful activity, the consciousness of doing good, peace of mind, and bright hope of a glorious destiny hereafter? Away with such a word, such a view, and such a thought! It is emphatically no sacrifice. Say rather it is a privilege. Anxiety, sickness, suffering or danger now and then, with a foregoing of the common conveniences and charities of this life, may make us pause and cause the spirit to waver and sink; but let this only be for a moment. All these are nothing when compared with the glory which shall hereafter be revealed in and for us. I never made a sacrifice. Of this we ought not talk when we remember the great sacrifice which He made who left His Father's throne on high to give Himself for us."

Connecting to the Story

One day in the barnyard, a hen grieved over the problem of hunger in the world was sharing her grave concern with the head hog. As they were discussing the problem, the hen came up with what she thought was an incredible idea. She suggested that every morning, she and the pig provide a ham and egg breakfast to anyone who was hungry. The pig looked immediately at the hen, and said, "Yeah, there is a flaw in your idea. See, for you, your idea only requires an offering, while for me, it requires total sacrifice.

Exercise: What is the difference between giving an offering and making a sacrifice and what is the relevance of this idea as it pertains to following Jesus?

The simple truth is that too many professing Christians are more like the hen than the hog. Like the hen, we are just sort of involved. We give a little here – and a little more there, but when following Jesus requires an actual sacrifice of our time, talents, treasures, and testimony – we are just not up to the ask. Yet Paul, in Romans 12:1-2, says that a life that truly honors and worships God requires each of us to become a living sacrifice that is holy and pleasing to God.

Question: *What is worship to you? What ideas and memories come to mind when you think of worship?*

Diving into the Story

What's It All About

In penning these words to the Roman Christians, Paul is calling them to a life of worship that encounters, experiences, and expresses God's will in their daily lives. Simply put, the highest form of worship is living as a living sacrifice unto God engaged in accomplishing God's will. In fact, whenever I read this text, I'm struck by the emphasis on God's will and how essential it is to the worship of God. Thus, it is God's will we experience His mercy. It is His will that we become a living sacrifice that is holy and pleasing to Him. It is His will that our lives are an act of worship. It is also God's will that we live by the economy of heaven instead of earth and that we live spiritually focused lives. Meaning, God has a plan and purpose for us, and when we find and follow His will, our lives serve as an act of worship that honors Him.

Understanding this reality, as we seek to honor God by seeking first His kingdom and righteousness, God works out His plan and purpose in us while allowing us the "freedom" to make choices – even though our sense of "free" will is held intently within His sovereignty. Thus, while we may make wrong choices along the way, we will never make one move outside of His Divine purview. So, God will never be fooled or surprised by our actions; yet at the same time, He can take our lives, including our mistakes, errors, and sins, and weave them into an amazing mosaic for His glory, our good – and if we cooperate with Him, for the good of other people too. Thus, essential to living a life that is pleasing to God is living a life that is in the center of His will.

Question: How do I discover and live God's will for my life? Even more, what is God's will?

The Big Idea
The ultimate act of worship is living an abandoned and pleasing life that experiences and accomplishes God's good, pleasing, and perfect will.

Christ in the Text
Jesus Christ is the sacrifice that makes it possible for every believer to be transformed by the renewing of their mind and to resist the pull of conformity to this world. In Christ, believers are changed to live a life of worship.

#1 Worship is a Matter of God's Will

I appeal to you therefore, brothers, by the mercies of God, to present your bodies as a living sacrifice, holy and acceptable to God, which is your spiritual worship. Do not be conformed to this world, but be transformed by the renewal of your mind, that by testing you may discern what is the will of God, what is good and acceptable and perfect.

Romans 12:1-2

1. Which aspect of God's Will is Romans 12:1-2 speaking about? How do you know?

2. What does God's Will being accomplished have to do with our personal worship?

3. What is God's perfect will? What is His permissive will? What role do aspects of God's Will play in His providential, prescriptive, and personal Will?

#2 Four Keys to Experiencing God's Will

I appeal to you therefore, brothers, by the mercies of God, to present your bodies as a living sacrifice, holy and acceptable to God, which is your spiritual worship. Do not be conformed to this world, but be transformed by the renewal of your mind, that by testing you may discern what is the will of God, what is good and acceptable and perfect.
Romans 12:1-2

(Surrender to God in Salvation, Sacrifice, Separation and Single-Mindedness)

1. In a world filled with multiple religions and spiritual pathways, why is Jesus so essential? How does a person surrender to God in salvation?

2. Why is being a living sacrifice so difficult? What does God really want and expect of us? What is the alternative to being a living sacrifice?

3. How does the world try to stuff us in its mold? What are some things we can do to ensure that we are sculpted by Christ instead of being stuffed into the world's mold?

4. Read Joshua 24:14-15. What does it mean to fear the Lord? What did Joshua mean by "do away with the gods your fathers served…?" What did Joshua mean when he said, "Choose for yourselves today whom you will serve? How does this request apply to us today?

👣 Diving Deeper

1. What is the biggest takeaway from this passage?

2. What are some ways you could apply this passage?

> *Is there a sin to avoid?*
> *Is there a promise to claim?*
> *Is there a command to obey?*
> *Is there an example to follow?*
> *Is there praise to give?*

3. What does sacrifice of self-sacrifice mean for you?

4. What will you apply specifically this week?

5. Who will hold you accountable this week to your response to Question 4?

What is worship? Worship is to feel in your heart and express in some appropriate manner a humbling but delightful sense of admiring awe and astonished wonder and overpowering love in the presence of that most ancient Mystery, that Majesty which philosophers call the First Cause, but which we call Our Father Which Are in Heaven.
~ A.W. Tozer

GROW Passages for Week 3

1. Exodus 20:2-6

2. 1 Chronicles 16:8-31

3. Isaiah 6:1-8

4. Acts 16:16-34

5. Romans 12:1-2

Session 4

Abide in the Word

2 Timothy 3:10-17

Eleanor Schmidt recalled a time when her doctor had recommended surgery and referred her to a specialist. She said, "Arriving early for my appointment, I found the door unlocked and the young surgeon, deeply engrossed in reading, behind the receptionist's desk. When he didn't hear me come in, I cleared my throat. Startled, he closed the book, which I recognized as a Bible. "Does reading the Bible help you before or after an operation?" I asked. My fears were dispelled by his soft, one-word answer: "During."

Life is hard enough trying to rely on personal philosophies, discerning for wisdom among the multitude of voices clamoring for our attention and the pressures of making the right decisions at all times. When there is only culture and books to give us counsel, we are hard-pressed to know what to do. However, God has not left us without his wisdom. Before we start our day, after we finish our day and during our day, we have access to God's wisdom and insights through the pages of his Word. The bible is filled with the story of God and his redemptive plan for humanity. In the bible there is wisdom to handle the most difficult situations and the most strenuous moments in life. Its pages are rich with meaning, instruction and encouragement. Its message is singular, in that, it speaks to the love of God revealed in Jesus Christ. The discipline of the disciple is to abide in the Word. Why? Because the Word is transferable, transformational and profitable to all who read, hear and obey it.

👣 Connecting to the Story

What is an idea, influence, or philosophy that has shaped cultural thinking over the past few decades? How has it changed the culture and how has it changed you?

👣 Diving into the Story

What It's All About
What you believe matters. What you believe and the convictions you possess, shape the way you live. The influences and influencers of a society can change the way people think. When thinking changes it filters into every fabric of humanity through reformed policies, laws, and behavior that become the new normal. The greatest influencer in a Christian's life must be Scripture. This is the lesson Paul is trying to teach Timothy, a young pastor and disciple of the Apostle Paul.

In his last letter, Paul uses this moment to remind Timothy that perilous days are coming (2 Tim. 3:1). There are coming days of apostasy where people are "always learning and never able to arrive at a knowledge of the truth" (2 Tim. 3:7). Paul tells Timothy that he must preach the word when the times are favorable and when they are not favorable (2 Tim. 4:2). The times that are not favorable are when "people will not endure sound teaching, but having itching ears they will accumulate for themselves teachers to suit their own passions and will turn away from listening to the truth and wander off into myths" (2 Tim. 4:3-4). With this in mind, Paul emphasizes the critical nature of Timothy's conviction for all Scripture. Without a firm grasp of Scripture or a firm belief in the gospel that has changed his life, Timothy does not have a chance to lead his church to the truth found only in Jesus Christ. Paul urges Timothy to continue in the faith he has learned from his grandmother, mother, and himself (2 Tim. 1:3-14). Paul points out that Jesus Christ has risen from the dead, and that message is not bound like he is in chains (2 Tim. 2:9). Given the reality of Christ's victory over death and fulfillment of prophecy, Paul confidently asserted under the Spirit's direction that "all Scripture is breathed out by God" (2 Tim. 3:16). The very thought that God breathed out his Word into the lives of people for their benefit is unimaginable. Paul tells Timothy that Scripture is profitable for teaching, reproof, correction, and training in righteousness for the purpose of the disciple's maturity and readiness to do every good work of God. Without Scripture, disciples cannot and will not grow to maturity, and without maturity, they are prey to heresy and the attacks of the enemy. Therefore, it is imperative to continue in the Word, know the saving power of the Word and be equipped with the transformative purpose of the Word.

The Big Idea
All Scripture has been given by God so that his disciples will believe it, obey it, and share it in every generation helping everyone who believes know the Lord and how to serve him.

Christ in the Text
Scripture is all about Jesus Christ. He is the authority of Scripture and the point of Scripture. Abiding in Christ is to abide in his word so that in every good work the disciple is fruitful.

#1 Abide in the Word Because it is Transferable

You, however, have followed my teaching, my conduct, my aim in life, my faith, my patience, my love, my steadfastness, my persecutions, and sufferings that happened to me at Antioch, at Iconium, and at Lystra – which persecutions I endured; yet from them all the Lord rescued me. Indeed, all who desire to live a godly life in Christ Jesus will be persecuted, while evil people and imposters will go on from bad to worse, deceiving and being deceived. But as for you, continue in what you have learned and have firmly believed, knowing from whom you learned it.

2 Timothy 3:10-14

1. Discuss the importance of transferring Scripture from one family member (or generation) to another.

2. What are ways you have seen this happen and what is the generational fruit that has been produced?

#2 Abide in the Word Because it is Transformational

And how from childhood you have been acquainted with the sacred writings, which are able to make you wise for salvation through faith in Christ Jesus.

2 Timothy 3:15

1. What did you learn as a child about the bible?

2. How did it impact and influence your decision to follow Christ?

3. How are you using the bible in your home with your family?

#3 Abide in the Word because it is Profitable

All Scripture is breathed out by God and profitable for teaching, for reproof, for correction, and for training in righteousness, that the man of God may be complete, equipped for every good work.
2 Timothy 3:16-17

1. How has the Word of God personally impacted your life?

2. How have you seen the four ways the bible works (teaching, reproof, correction and training) influence your relationships, family and career?

👣 Diving Deeper

1. What is the biggest takeaway from this passage?

2. What are some ways you could apply this passage?

Is there a sin to avoid?
Is there a promise to claim?
Is there a command to obey?
Is there an example to follow?
Is there praise to give?

3. How does the bible fit into your daily routine?

4. What will you apply specifically this week?

5. Who will hold you accountable this week to your response to Question 4?

> "I am a man of one book."
> ~ John Wesley

👣 GROW Passages for Week 4

1. Psalm 1:1-6; 119:9-16

2. Hebrews 4:11-13

3. Psalm 19:7-11

4. 2 Timothy 2:15; 3:16-17

5. James 1:19-27

Session 5

Living a Spirit-Empowered Life

Ephesians 3:14-19

There is a story about a lumber jack who went into a hardware store to buy another axe. While he was there, he discovered something new to him: the power chainsaw. The owner convinced him that he could cut down twice as many trees with much less effort. The lumber jack excitedly went purchased one. A couple days later, the lumber jack came to the hardware store and threw the saw down on the counter. He said, "This thing is a piece of junk! I used to cut down three or four trees a day. I haven't been able to get through one with this saw!" The store owner looked confused, picked up the chainsaw and pulled the strong. "VROOOM!" The lumber jack said, "What's that noise?"

Too often, Christians live with the reality of the Holy Spirit but not in the power of the Holy Spirit. Until we access his power through obedience, prayer, meditation in his Word and joining in community with his church, we will fail to be strengthened with his Spirit. The Holy Spirit works in the life of believers to live the empowering life of Jesus Christ through them, and to make us ambassadors of his grace for a world in need of the redemptive love of Christ. Paul prays for every believer to be consumed by the comprehensive love of Jesus until they are filled with all the fullness of God. When Christians walk in that fullness, there is no room to be filled with the evil of the world. A Christian who walks in the power of the Spirit is a powerful force for God's kingdom and a light that shines brightly in the darkness.

👣 Connecting to the Story

What do you tend to pray for the most? What is the most important prayer you could pray for your family?

👣 Diving into the Story

What It's All About

In his commentary on *Ephesians*, John R.W. Stott wrote: "One of the best ways to discover a Christian's chief anxieties and ambitions is to study the content of his prayers and the intensity with which he prays them."[iii] What we pray about gives a window in our soul to the things we think about the most and cherish the most. Praying for our own needs is acceptable and expected, but if our prayers are dominated by them, then it reveals a self-centered focus. Prayer must be a balance between the personal and the relational, between the temporal and the eternal. In the prayer Paul prays for the Ephesians, Paul pours out his heart and soul to God. In the first part of the letter, Paul lays out the doctrine of grace through faith and mystery of the gospel, "that Gentiles are fellow heirs, members of the same body, and partakers of the promise in Christ Jesus through the gospel" (Ephesians 3:6). Now, Paul prays for the Christians with earnestness and power. His heart's desire is for them to know the Spirit-empowered life that fill them with God's love so that they are strengthened for whatever comes their way.

What Paul is using is the discipline of intercessory prayer. It means praying for someone else on behalf of the person, in many cases, when the situation is so extreme that they cannot pray for themselves. The

Holy Spirit does this on our behalf. Paul teaches in Romans 8 that "the Spirit helps us in our weakness. For we do not know what to pray for as we ought, but the Spirit himself intercedes for us with groanings too deep for words" (Romans 8:26). The characteristic of a Spirit-empowered church and a Spirit-empowered life is their willingness to intercede. It means a deep love for their family in Christ. It reveals a hunger for them to be equipped with all the saints to build up the body of Christ, "until we all attain to the unity of the faith and of the knowledge of the Son of God, to mature manhood, to the measure of the stature of the fullness of Christ, so that we may no longer be children, tossed to and fro by the waves and carried about by every wind of doctrine, by human cunning, by craftiness in deceitful schemes" (Eph. 4:12-14). Intercessory praying is also looking out for the interests of others as we think about their spiritual progress and needs rather than hyper-focusing on our own (Phil. 2:3-4). When this happens, it brings unity to the church no matter how strained some might be relationally within the church. As Dietrich Bonhoeffer wrote in *Life Together*, "I can no longer condemn or hate a brother for whom I pray; no matter how much trouble he causes me. His face, that hitherto may have been strange and intolerable to me, is transformed in intercession into the countenance of a brother for whom Christ died."[iv]

With intercessory prayer being at the forefront of this lesson, the focus is on what should be prayed for the church if the church is going to continue to be a Spirit-empowered influence in the community and in their families.

The Big Idea
Paul prays for God's people to be Spirit-empowered so they can be rooted in Christ and know the fullness of God revealed in the knowledge of Christ's comprehensive love for his church.

Christ in the Text

Paul prays that the church knows the love of Christ so comprehensively that they are filled with all the fullness of God. He wants the people of God to be known as Christ followers who are radically committed to Jesus no matter what happens to them in life.

#1 To Be Strengthened with Power through His Spirit (3:14-16)

For this reason I bow my knees before the Father, from whom every family in heaven and on earth is named, that according to the riches of his glory he may grant you to be strengthened with power through his spirit in the inner being.

Eph. 3:14-16

1. What is the purpose of Paul's prayer?

2. Why is this an important prayer for Christians to pray for one another?

3. How do you see the power of the Spirit strengthening you inwardly?

4. What difference is he making in your life daily?

#2 To Be a Dwelling of Christ through Faith (3:17a)

So that Christ may dwell in your hearts through faith.
Ephesians 3:17a

1. What is it about the indwelling of Christ in our hearts that moves us to greater depths with Christ? Think about the reality of Christ constantly residing in every part of your life.

2. How does this reality shape the way you live? How different would your life look if he physically resided with you?

#3 To Be Fully Aware of God's Comprehensive Love for You (3:17b-19)

That you, being rooted and grounded in love, may have strength to comprehend with all the saints what is the breadth and length and height and depth, and to know the love Christ that surpasses knowledge, that you may be filled with all the fullness of God.
Ephesians 3:17b-19

1. Discuss the implications of the all-encompassing nature of God's love.

2. How are you experiencing it daily?

3. How does it impact the way you live with and love others?

👣 Diving Deeper

1. What is the biggest takeaway from this passage?

2. What are some ways you could apply this passage?

> *Is there a sin to avoid?*
> *Is there a promise to claim?*
> *Is there a command to obey?*
> *Is there an example to follow?*
> *Is there praise to give?*

3. How does the love of God work its way out in your daily routine of living?

4. What will you apply specifically this week?

5. Who will hold you accountable this week to your response to Question 4?

Thomas Goodwin, a Puritan theologian, when writing from John 14:1-13, speaks about the reason Christ truly loves us. He writes, "It is as if [Jesus] had said, "The truth is, I cannot live without you, I shall never be quiet till I have you where I am, that so we may never part again; that is the reason of it. Heaven shall not hold me, nor my Father's company, if I have not you with me, my heart is set upon you; and if I have any glory, you shall have part of it."

GROW Passages for Week 5

1. Matthew 6:5-16

2. Philippians 4:4-9

3. Matthew 7:7-12

4. Ephesians 3:14-19

5. 1 John 5:13-15

Session 6

Trust Applied

Proverbs 3:5-10

In his book, *Ruthless Trust*, Brandon Manning tells the story of John Kavanaugh, a famous ethicist, who went to Calcutta in search of Mother Teresa and some words of wisdom. Manning writes, "He went for three months to work at "the house of the dying" to find out how best he could spend the rest of his life. When he met Mother Teresa, he asked her to pray for him. "What do you want me to pray for?" she replied. He then uttered the request he had carried thousands of miles: "Clarity. Pray that I have clarity." "No," Mother Teresa answered, "I will not do that." When he asked her why, she said, "Clarity is the last thing you are clinging to and must let go of." When Kavanaugh said that she always seemed to have clarity, the very kind of clarity he was looking for, Mother Teresa laughed and said: "I have never had clarity; what I have always had is trust. So, I will pray that you trust God."

Trust is relying on promises from someone who fulfills their word. Trust is needed in about every situation in life. Without trust, people cannot move forward with their plans, partner with others on projects or grow relationally and emotionally. Stephen Covey said, "Trust is the glue of life. It's the most essential ingredient in effective communication. It's the foundational principle that holds all relationships." Trusting others explicitly is like finding the holy grail. We long for it and search for it, and when we find it, we hold on to it with the firmest grip. But nothing breaks our heart like broken trust. Broken trust is the result of living in a fallen world with fallen people.

That is why trusting in God is essential to life, because God has always and will always keep his promises. God cannot be God without explicit trust. He is forever faithful. True wisdom is found when a person trusts their life to someone they cannot see but knows will never let them down.

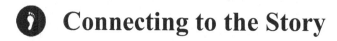 Connecting to the Story

What are some things people trust in today for their significance, security, and sanity? What are some "alternate" gods that creep into your life from time to time?

Diving into the Story

What It's All About
Nothing is more important in the Christian life than trust in the Lord. Hebrews 11:6 says, "And without faith (trust) it is impossible to please him, for whoever would draw near to God must believe that he exists and that rewards those who seek him." The Lord does not require a half-hearted devotion but one in which you lean on him with every fiber of your soul. Trust in the Lord is how believers gain wisdom for every moment in life. Believers trust in the Lord with all confidence while intentionally allowing and inviting the Lord into every decision and thought of their life. When the believer trusts in the Lord wholeheartedly, the Lord removes obstructions from their path and gives instructions for circumstantial living. Following the principle of trust, the Lord calls the believer to lean completely on the Lord, find their wisdom in God alone, fear the Lord alone, and turn away from evil. Then, demonstrating wholehearted trust, the believer honors the

Lord with the best of their wealth producing a life blessed by the promises of God that result in guidance, healing, and prosperity.

In Tim and Kathy Keller's devotional on *Proverbs*, she writes, "Our culture tells us to submit everything to our understanding, to question everything including the Bible. But everyone must choose something to not question. Modern people don't question the right and ability to question everything. So everyone is living by faith in some ultimate authority. Proverbs calls us to make it God's word, not our reason and intuition. The Bible can guide you in all your ways, even when there is not a specific verse for every life situation. As you immerse yourself in the Bible story of a personal God who made us and saved us for a relationship with him, it makes every part of life – how you spend your money, relate to people, allocate your time, and see yourself – look different than if you didn't believe the story. Then wisdom grows as you live daily life shaped by the biblical narrative and vine realities."[v]

The Big Idea
To truly gain God's wisdom, grow in understanding for every situation of life, and experience life as God created, Christians must wholeheartedly trust in the Lord.

Christ in the Text
Jesus Christ is the wisdom of God, and in him, we know how to navigate the paths of life, how to live in the freedom of redemption, and enjoy the fruits of our obedience to him.

#1 The Principle of Trust Applied (Proverbs 3:5)

Trust in the Lord with all your heart, and do not lean on your own understanding.

Proverbs 3:5

1. What is your best way to think about trust?

2. What does it look like to trust the Lord with all your heart?

3. Is this a challenge for you at times?

4. What is the difference between leaning on the knowledge God provides through education and trusting in the Lord?

#2 The Practice of Trust Applied (Proverbs 3:6, 7, & 9)

In all your ways acknowledge him, and he will make straight your paths. Be not wise in your own eyes; fear the Lord, and turn away from evil. Honor the Lord with your wealth and with the first fruits of all your produce.

Proverbs 3:6-7, 9

1. How is acknowledgement of the Lord different than submission to the Lord?

2. What does it mean practically in your life to submit to the Lord in your character, conduct, and currency?

#3 The Promise of Trust Applied (Proverbs 3:6, 8, 10)

In all your ways acknowledge him, and he will make straight your paths. It will be healing to your flesh and refreshment to your bones. Then your barns will be filled with plenty,
and your vats will be bursting with wine.

Proverbs 3:6, 8, 10

1. How does the promise of God's direction in your life influence your submission to his will?

2. In what way is trusting in the Lord healing and refreshment? How does it affect your physically?

3. What does it mean that God will prosper us when we trust him? What are some ways that could be manifested in our lives?

Diving Deeper

1. What is the biggest takeaway from this passage?

2. What are some ways you could apply this passage?

   Is there a sin to avoid?
   Is there a promise to claim?
   Is there a command to obey?
   Is there an example to follow?
   Is there praise to give?

3. What is your greatest challenge to trust the Lord with all your heart?

4. What will you apply specifically this week?

5. Who will hold you accountable this week to your response to Question 4?

"People…think faith is a big electric blanket, when of course it is the cross…You arrive at enough certainty to be able to make your way, but it is making it in darkness. Don't expect faith to clear things up for you. It is trust, not certainty."
~ Flannery O'Connor

GROW Passages for Week 6

1. Matthew 6:19-34

2. Proverbs 3:5-10

3. Matthew 7:24-27

4. Malachi 3:6-12

5. Matthew 25:14-30

Session 7

Ready to Tell

1 Peter 3:8-17

Howard Hendricks, former professor at Dallas Theological was famous for saying, "In the midst of a generation screaming for answers, Christians are stuttering." Nothing quenches the witness of a Christian like a life lived contradictory to the message. When the church does not reflect the values of God's kingdom through unity in relationships, brotherly love, compassion and humility, then Christians will not be able to speak into the culture, no matter how educated they might be. One day there was an explosion in a small-town factory. In the blast, a factory worker was severely burned. His friend and coworker had been knocked back but came away unscathed. He ran over to his friend but quickly realized that he was not going to make it. The injured man was lightly breathing with his eyes slightly open. He spoke with his friend who amazingly told him to tell his family that he loved him. Within several minutes, he was gone. The incident haunted the man for weeks, but not because of the trauma he experienced. Finally, he went to speak to his pastor. The man confessed that the one thing on his mind was that his friend was ready to enter eternity. He knew the man did not believe in Jesus. The pastor asked, "What stopped you from sharing the gospel with him in that moment." The man responded, "My life closed my lips."

Christians can learn Gospel outlines, formulas, apologetic arguments and know how to recite multiple bible verses, but if they are not prepared to share Christ with their life, the greatest message ever told will fall silent. Peter calls the church to have a clear conscience when living for Christ. He tells them that they will be slandered for doing right, but make sure they are not slandered for doing wrong. Christians will be ready to tell the Good News of Jesus Christ when their relationships are unified and their life is characterized by the character and conduct of Christ.

Connecting to the Story

What threatens to disturb the harmony of your church? What can be done to restore or maintain harmony?

Diving into the Story

What's It All About?
Warren Wiersbe wrote, "Hope is not a sedative; it is a shot of adrenaline, a blood transfusion. Like an anchor, our hope in Christ stabilizes us in the storms of life; but unlike an anchor, our hope moves us forward, it does not hold us back." In the words of Peter, we learn that living life involves spiritual growth verified by positive daily relationships and activities. General Douglas MacArther focused on a similar perspective. He wrote "Life is a lively process of becoming. If you haven't added to your interest during the past year; if you are thinking the same thoughts, relating the same personal experiences, having the same predicable reactions, then rigor mortis of the personality has set in."

Relationships! We cannot go very far in life before we realize how important relationships are. Peter puts an exclamation point on the believer's relationship with God the Father. This relationship is never far from his mind or pen. He also carefully underlines the importance of positive relationships with one another. Paul's premise is that those who have a secure relationship with the Father through Jesus Christ are now on a path of spiritual growth and development.

One of the crucial growth points on this path is how we can reflect positively the relationship with God. This reflection is not simply to be relegated to a verbal testimony or witness, but it takes form as we live day to day among our fellow Christians and before those who do not know Christ. Certain attitudes and actions need to be surrendered from the believer's pattern of living, lest our testimony be lost to others. We have a responsibility to live out a submissive relationship toward the government and to employers, but most importantly, we are to demonstrate the love of Jesus.

The point cannot be missed: relationships inside and outside the church are vital to the witness of Christians. It's one thing to be a model of positive relationships at church. It's another to be a model of Christ-like behavior to those outside the church. Half-hearted efforts for harmony are not satisfactory. Life in the church family requires diligence from every member. A similar effort is needed to respond and act appropriately to those outside the body of Christ, particularly when they speak against you. In every situation one thing should be uppermost in our minds: the continuing opportunity to present the gospel of Jesus Christ to those who stand in need. We must not short-circuit any opportunities to do so by our misguided and inappropriate responses and actions.

The Big Idea
Live in harmony with one another; return good for evil, and you will inherit a blessing from God.

Christ in the Text

Where do we find the example of a harmonious relationship? Jesus Christ. Jesus came to reconcile man back to God. Christ is the embodiment of love, sympathy, compassion, and humility. Only if you have a strong foundation in Jesus can you have harmony in your other relationships.

#1 Called to Blessing, Relationships in the Church (3:8-12)

Finally, all of you, have unity of mind, sympathy, brotherly love, a tender heart, and a humble mind. Do not repeat evil for evil or reviling for reviling, but on the contrary, blessed, four to this you were called, that you may obtain a blessing. For 'Whoever desires to love life and see good days, let him keep his tongue from evil and his lips from speaking deceit; let him turn away from evil and do good; thank let him seek peace and pursue it. For the eyes of the Lord are on the righteous, and his ears are open to the prayer. But the face of the Lord is against those who do evil'.

1 Peter 3:8-12

1. What threatens to disturb the harmony of your church?

2. What can be done to restore or maintain harmony?

#2 Suffering for Right and Relationships with People Outside the Church (1 Pet. 3:13-17)

Now who is there to harm you if you are zealous for what is good? But even if you should suffer for righteousness' sake, you will be blessed. Have no fear of them, nor be troubled, but in your hearts honor Christ the Lord as holy, always being prepared to make a defense to anyone who ask you for a reason for the hope that is in you; yet do it with gentleness and respect, having a good conscience, so that when you are slandered, those who revile your good behavior in Christ may be put to shame. For it is better to suffer for doing good, if that should be God's will, than for doing evil.

1 Peter 3:13-17

1. How is your suffering or pain related to your salvation?

2. What does it look like for you to honor Christ in your heart when being persecuted for doing good?

3. How are you preparing yourself to make a defense for the hope you have in you?

#3 To Be Fully Aware of God's Comprehensive Love for You (3:17b-19)

That you, being rooted and grounded in love, may have strength to comprehend with all the saints what is the breadth and length and height and depth, and to know the love Christ that surpasses knowledge, that you may be filled with all the fullness of God.
Ephesians 3:17b-19

1. Discuss the implications of the all-encompassing nature of God's love.

2. How are you experiencing it daily?

3. How does it impact the way you live with and love others?

👣 Diving Deeper

1. What is the biggest takeaway from this passage?

2. What are some ways you could apply this passage?

   Is there a sin to avoid?
   Is there a promise to claim?
   Is there a command to obey?
   Is there an example to follow?
   Is there praise to give?

3. In what way are you blessed even when you suffer for what is right?

4. What will you apply specifically this week?

5. Who will hold you accountable this week to your response to Question 4?

Richard Baxter writes, "How few know how to deal with an ignorant, worldly man, for his conversion! And to get within him and win upon him; to suit our speech to his condition and temper; to choose the meatiest subjects, and follow them with a holy mixture of seriousness, and terror, and love, and meekness, and evangelical allurements – oh! who is fit for such a thing?"

GROW Passages for Week 7

1. Matthew 4:18-22

2. Romans 10:14-17

3. 1 Peter 3:8-17

4. Acts 1:1-11

5. 2 Corinthians 5:14-21

Session 8

The Spiritual Household of God

1 Peter 2:4-10

In his book, *Waiting on God*, Wayne Stiles writes, "I'm convinced some company today could make a killing if it had the guts to market dysfunctional greeting cards. Most birthday or holiday cards gush with flowery sentiments such as, "To the greatest father in the world," or, "Mom, you are my best friend." Yeah, well, what if they weren't? What if your dad was an angry jerk and your mother abused you? What if your brother backstabbed you and stole the inheritance? Where are the greeting cards for reality? Just once I'd like to see a card that reads, "Mom, you blew it . . . but I love you anyway. Happy Mother's Day." It'll never happen. Even if such cards existed, few people would have the cruelty to send them. So instead, we shop for cards that are blank inside and do our best to scrawl some positive words. There are no easy solutions. Only godly ones. After all, on some level we all deserve to open dysfunctional envelopes since we each contribute our own family defects." Families are never perfect because we are all a part of one. The family is God is not perfect either, except for the One who is the Head of the family.

The spiritual household of God is made up of people from various backgrounds but all with the common virtue of utter depravity. However, each person who has come to Jesus Christ in faith for their salvation is a part of a spiritual building or spiritual family that has Christ has the chief cornerstone of the foundation. In contrast to those who have stumbled over Christ in their disbelief, Christ followers are a chosen race, a royal priesthood, a holy nation and a people for his own possession. Our singular purpose is to proclaim the excellencies of Jesus who called us out of darkness into his marvelous light. We belong to Jesus! We belong to the household of God! Our identity and purpose are set in Christ and for Christ. The real work of the kingdom is to submit ourselves to the master builder who intends to place each stone in its position and erect a massive spiritual structure for the glory of God and the proclamation of his majesty. You are one of those stones, in indeed, you are in Christ.

Connecting to the Story

What process is God undertaking in the lives of believers?

Behold, how good and how pleasant it is for brethren to dwell together in unity!" Psalm 133:1 The message in this Psalm can be considered a cornerstone of what Peter is telling us in this lesson. We are to be a Holy Priesthood! What does it mean to be a Holy Priesthood? As we strive to be worthy of this calling there are several issues we must address. The life-changing power of the Word of God must affect our lives as Christians. Reborn children of God should exhibit their new life in their day-to-day conduct. Believers ought to exhibit a different quality of life, marked by continuous spiritual growth. The unity of church members will be seen by the unbelievers and become a part of our living testimonies. Believers in Jesus Christ have experienced a taste of God's grace in our lives. God's grace is no excuse for us to behave as we please. The goodness and grace of God should be our greatest incentives for spiritual growth and progress. We are called to "take up our cross and follow Him." As we answer this call, we should look at ourselves as "Christian Soldiers "and our unity gives us the strength we must have to be successful in progressing forward spiritually.

Have you ever been on a trip with a group when one person in the group complained about everything and was generally disagreeable? If one person is out of step, it tends to ruin the trip for everyone. On the other hand, nothing is more enjoyable than sharing the adventures of life with friends of a like mind and kindred spirit. God expects us to live in unity with other believers. That does not mean that we are all to be "cookie-cutter" Christians who agree on everything. There is a vast difference between uniformity and unity. Someone has said that you can tie two cats' tails together and have union, but you sure won't have unity.

Maybe the best illustration of dwelling in unity is a loving family. Each family member is different in his or her temperaments, talents, and perhaps even tastes. Yet, as family, we share a common heritage and values. We are to relate to other Christians as family, not only because we share the same parentage and heritage but also the hope for the future. For a family to function the way God intends, we have to be willing to yield our rights on occasion and to be quick to give and receive forgiveness. The same is true for our spiritual family, the church. God loves it when His Kids "dwell together in unity."

The Big Idea
Live godly lives because God is building you into a spiritual house through Christ. He has made you a royal priesthood to be a positive example and witness to others. Therefore, respond properly to human authorities as well as to unjust suffering in your lives.

Christ in the Text
The Spirit of Christ was present in the Hebrew prophets pointing them to the suffering of Christ and the glory that followed His suffering. Christ is like a lamb without defect or blemish. His precious blood redeems believers from their futile ways. Believers can expect to suffer as He suffered and anticipate the joy of His coming in glory.

#1 The Steps Toward Being a Spiritual Sacrifice in the Household of God (1 Pet. 2:4-10)

As you come to him, a living stone rejected by men but in the sight of God chosen and precious, you yourselves like living stones are being built up as a spiritual house, to be a holy priesthood, to offer spiritual sacrifices acceptable to God through Jesus Christ. For it stands in Scripture: "Behold, I am laying in Zion a stone a cornerstone chosen and precious, and whoever believes in him will not be put to shame." So the honor is for you who believe, but for those who do not believe, "The stone that the builders rejected has become the cornerstone," and "A stone of stumbling, and a rock of offense." They stumble because they disobey the word, as they were destined to do. But you are a chosen race, a royal priesthood, a holy nation, a people for his own possession, that you may proclaim the excellencies of him who called you out of darkness into his marvelous light. Once you were not a people, but now you are God's people; once you had not received mercy, but now you have received mercy.

1 Peter 2:4-10

1. What does it mean to be a holy priesthood? To offer spiritual sacrifices acceptable to God?

2. Why is Jesus a stone of stumbling to those who do not believe?

3. How does it change the way you live knowing you are chosen (2:9)?

2 The Identifiers of the Spiritual Sacrifice in the Household of God (1 Pet. 2:1-10)

So put away all malice and all deceit and hypocrisy and envy and all slander. Like newborn infants, long for the pure spiritual milk, that by it you may grow up into salvation – if indeed you have tasted that the Lord is good. As you come to him, a living stone rejected by men but in the sight of God chosen and precious, you yourselves like living stones are being built up as a spiritual house, to be a holy priesthood, to offer spiritual sacrifices acceptable to God through Jesus Christ. For it stands in Scripture: "Behold, I am laying in Zion a stone a cornerstone chosen and precious, and whoever believes in him will not be put to shame." So the honor is for you who believe, but for those who do not believe, "The stone that the builders rejected has become the cornerstone," and "A stone of stumbling, and a rock of offense." They stumble because they disobey the word, as they were destined to do. But you are a chosen race, a royal priesthood, a holy nation, a people for his own possession, that you may proclaim the excellencies of him who called you out of darkness into his marvelous light. Once you were not a people, but now you are God's people; once you had not received mercy, but now you have received mercy.

1 Peter 2:4-10

1. Why does Peter describe Jesus as a cornerstone?

2. What are the two responses to this stone, and the outcome of each response?

👣 Diving Deeper

1. What is the biggest takeaway from this passage?

2. What are some ways you could apply this passage?

   Is there a sin to avoid?
   Is there a promise to claim?
   Is there a command to obey?
   Is there an example to follow?
   Is there praise to give?

3. With do you need to proclaim the excellencies of him who called you out of darkness into his marvelous light?

4. What will you apply specifically this week?

5. Who will hold you accountable this week to your response to Question 4?

Robert Murray McCheyne wrote, "It is the voice of Christ that wakens the dead soul. Jesus speaks through the Bible, through ministers, through providences. His voice can reach the dead. He quickeneth whom He will. They that hear, live."

GROW Passages for Week 8

1. Acts 2:42-47

2. Hebrews 10:19-25

3. Romans 12:3-8

4. Ephesians 2:11-22

5. 1 Peter 2:4-10

Session 9

Loving Beyond Limits

John 13:1-17

Selflessness is a rarity! Few want to take the back seat to others, especially when they think they deserve more. C.S. Kirkendall, Jr. writes about the selflessness of Edmund Halley (who would eventually go on to predict a returning comet that bears his name). He writes, "Every young student knows of Isaac Newton's famed encounter with a falling apple. Newton discovered and introduced the laws of gravity in the 1600s, which revolutionized astronomical studies. But few know that if it weren't for Edmund Halley, the world might never have learned from Newton. It was Halley who challenged Newton to think through his original notions. Halley corrected Newton's mathematical errors and prepared geometrical figures to support his discoveries. Halley coaxed the hesitant Newton to write his great work, *Mathematical Principles of Natural Philosophy*. Halley edited and supervised the publication, and actually financed its printing even though Newton was wealthier and easily could have afforded the printing costs. Historians call it one of the most selfless examples in the annals of science."

When you look at selfless acts, you could look to John the Baptist who said, "Jesus must increase and I must decrease." Or, you could look to Barnabas who took the back seat to Paul as they planted multiple churches. Maybe you think about soldiers who have fallen on live grenades to save their platoon. You might think about a parent who sacrificed everything to make sure you had what you needed to succeed and thrive. Every selfless act is one of love, courage and compassion. Of all the selfless acts ever committed, none could match the selfless act of Jesus Christ dying in humanity's place which no one deserved. But just before, Jesus shows them how much he loves them and how to love others by washing their feet. Jesus always loved beyond limits and calls his followers to do the same every day.

 ## Connecting to the Story

What has been one of the greatest expressions of love you have seen demonstrated and what impact did it make on your life?

 ## Diving into the Story

What It's All About
At the Passover, people would celebrate the Seder meal and then there would be an address to those in attendance. John records something altogether different and priceless. James Boice, reflecting on this passage says, "Nowhere in the entire Bible does the child of God feel that he is walking on more holy ground."[vi] John is the only Gospel writer that does not mention the Lord's Supper. It's not that he did not think it was important, but John was more concerned with meaning than with ceremony.

In the wake of the disciple's argument over who would be the greatest, as recorded in the Synoptic Gospels (Matthew, Mark, and Luke), Jesus performs a duty of enormous humility and significance that must have put everything that night into perspective. This point of emphasis is minor to the major emphasis Jesus gives of his love for his disciples who are in the world. In that culture, to see a demonstration of the teaching was much more effective than a lecture. Jesus loved his disciples, but it was not enough to tell them, they needed to see and experience his love. The intimacy and personal nature of the moment were a variance from the mass ministry Jesus had undertaken over the last three years. This moment was reserved for his disciples. They had walked with him, slept on the same ground, watched his miracles, and struggled together for the meaning of his mission.

With the enemy, Satan, already in their midst weaving his influence into Judas Iscariot, Jesus disregards the attack to show that there is something that rises above everything – love! John also points out that while Jesus is about to stoop down to wash their feet, his rightful place is much higher because he is aligned with the Father in a work of redemption on the cross. It's in that sovereign, lofty position of Redeemer and Savior that Jesus kneels to serve his disciples. In that moment, Jesus is living his words in Mark 10:45 "For even the Son of Man came not to be served but to serve, and to give his life as a ransom for many." The heart of Jesus' mission would be to serve, in that, his work of redemption on the cross was to serve all of humanity. You could say that the entirety of Jesus' mission was about loving others with words and deeds. The disciples would need this to move past their self-centeredness and the temptation to look beyond people if the people could not in turn help them. Jesus did not want his disciples to believe for a minute that life was "tit for tat". Jesus loved them despite their failures and flaws. He showed them how, why, and who they were to love. It was a lesson they would never forget and would take with them into the rest of their life as they launched the greatest movement of grace and truth in human history. Every disciple has the same calling, to live and love authentically.

In his book, *A Trip Around the Sun: Turning Your Everyday Life into the Adventure of a Lifetime,* Mark Batterson writes these simple words: "If you want to impact someone's life, love them when they least expect it and least deserve it."[vii] In this passage, Jesus gives you how to make the biggest impact on a person when they least expect it or least observe it.

The Big Idea
In a world rebelling against their Creator and lost in self-centeredness, Jesus exemplified love beyond limits through his character and conduct, giving his disciples and us a model of selflessness that could and must be replicated in a world desperately searching for true love.

Christ in the Text
Jesus Christ demonstrated his love toward sinners and transformed them in every way. His commitment to changing lives came from his deep love for people and desire for those who followed him to serve others with the love that had been poured into their hearts from him. This moment with his disciples served to show us true love and how we must go to all people with the love of Christ.

#1 Jesus Shows You How to Love (John 13:1-5)

Now before the Feast of the Passover, when Jesus knew that his hour had come to depart out of this world to the Father, having loved his own who were in the world, he loved them to the end. During supper, when the devil had already put it in the heart of Judas Iscariot, Simon's son, to betray him, Jesus, knowing that the Father had given all things into his hands, and that he had come from God and was going back to God, rose from supper. He laid aside his outer garments, and taking a towel, tied it around his waist. Then he poured water into basin and began to wash his disciple's feet and to wipe them with the towel that was wrapped around him

John 13:1-5

1. What impresses you about the actions of Jesus in light of his deity?

2. How does this challenge you in light of your humanity?

#2 Jesus Shows You Why You Love (John 13:6-11)

He came to Simon Peter, who said to him, 'Lord, do you wash my feet?' Jesus answered him, 'What I am doing you do not understand now, but afterward you will understand.' Peter said to him, 'You shall never wash my feet.' Jesus answered him, 'If I do not wash you, you have no share with me.' Simon Peter said to him, 'Lord, not my feet only but also my hands and my head.' Jesus said to him, 'The one who has bathed does not need to wash, except for his feet, but is completely clean, but not every one of you.' For he knew who was to betray him; that was why he said, 'Not all of you are clean.'

John 13:6-11

1. What is the motivation for love?

2. How does it get misused?

3. How does the work of Jesus Christ in you empower the way you love others?

#3 Jesus Shows You Who You Love (John 13:12-17)

When he had washed their feet and put on his outer garments and resumed his place, he said to them, "Do you understand what I have done to you? You call me Teacher and Lord, and you were right, for so I am. If I then, your Lord and Teacher, have washed your feet, you also ought to wash one another's feet. For I have given you an example, that you also should do just as I have done to you. Truly, truly, I say to you, a servant is not greater than his master, nor is a messenger greater than the one who sent him. If you know these things, blessed are you if you do them.

John 13:12-17

1. If God has sent you to love others, how and who has he sent you love this week?

2. What is your group doing to show that love to one another and to this community?

Diving Deeper

1. What is the biggest takeaway from this passage?

2. What are some ways you could apply this passage?

Is there a sin to avoid?
Is there a promise to claim?
Is there a command to obey?
Is there an example to follow?
Is there praise to give?

3. What is your greatest challenge in showing practical and intentional love to others?

4. What will you apply specifically this week?

5. Who will hold you accountable this week to your response to Question 4?

"If you want to impact someone's life, love them when they least expect it and least deserve it."
Mark Batterson, *A Trip Around the Sun: Turning Your Everyday Life into the Adventure of a Lifetime*,

---

GROW Passages for Week 9

1. John 13:1-17

2. Ephesians 2:1-10

3. 1 Samuel 12:19-25

4. Luke 10:25-37

5. Mark 10:35-45

Session 10

Hiding God's Word

Psalm 119:9-16

In his book, *The Wonders of the Work of God*, Robert Sumner writes, "A man in Kansas City was severely injured in an explosion. The victim's face was badly disfigured, and he lost his eyesight as well as both hands. He was just a new Christian, and one of his greatest disappointments was that he could no longer read the Bible. Then he heard about a lady in England who read braille with her lips. Hoping to do the same, he sent for some books of the Bible in braille. Much to his dismay, however, he discovered that the nerve endings in his lips had been destroyed by the explosion. One day, as he brought one of the braille pages to his lips, his tongue happened to touch a few of the raised characters and he could feel them. Like a flash he thought, I can read the Bible using my tongue."[viii] Sumner later said that the man "read" through the entire bible four times. The way we treasure God's Word in our hearts is by reading, reflecting, applying, and sharing it. When we guard our ways to live a life pleasing to the Lord, we take God's Word and make it the focal point of our affections.

Connecting to the Story

How do you measure what truly occupies the affections of your heart?

🦶 Diving into the Story

What It's All About
Psalm 119:9-16 is a short paragraph about the key for a person to keep his way pure before the Lord. The Psalmist uses "a young man" to contextualize the teaching on the importance of hiding God's Word in our hearts. The younger we are, the more immature and in need of instruction. He is not saying that getting older in years makes us wiser, but that treasuring God's Word is the way to guard our hearts against those things that create havoc in our lives. The writer lays out the principle in verse 9, the pursuit in verse 10, and the practical ways to apply God's Word in verses 11-16.

The Big Idea
Treasuring and applying God's Word are the keys to having and maintaining a heart that seeks God's holiness in every area of life.

Christ in the Text
Jesus Christ is the Word of God in whom every believer delights and seeks. When we treasure God's Word in our hearts, Christ is proclaimed through our character and conduct.

#1 The Principle (Psalm 119:9)

How can a young man keep his way pure? By guarding it according to your word.

Psalm 119:9

1. What is the implication of the Psalmist calling out 'young men'?

2. How does God's Word give us the tools to keep our lives from falling prey to the lies of the enemy?

#2 The Pursuit (Psalm 119:10)

With my whole heart I seek you; let me not wander from your commandments!

Psalm 119:10

1. What does your life look like when you are wholeheartedly pursuing God?

2. What does it look like when you are half-heartedly pursuing God?

3. How does each impact your marriage, your parenting, and your witness to others?

#3 The Practice (Psalm 119:11-16)

I have stored up your word in my heart, that I might not sin against you. Blessed are you, O Lord; teach me your statutes! With my lips I declare all the rules of your mouth. In the way of your testimonies, I delight as much as in all riches. I will meditate on your precepts and fix my eyes on your ways. I will delight in your statutes; I will not forget your word.

Psalm 119:11-16

1. For what amount would you deny yourself to ever hear or read God's Word again?

2. What roles does the bible play in your everyday life?

Diving Deeper

1. What is the biggest takeaway from this passage?

2. What are some ways you could apply this passage?

   Is there a sin to avoid?
   Is there a promise to claim?
   Is there a command to obey?
   Is there an example to follow?
   Is there praise to give?

3. Describe your daily or weekly routine with the bible?

4. What will you apply specifically this week?

5. Who will hold you accountable this week to your response to Question 4?

To *know* the Word of God, to *live* the Word of God, to *preach* the Word, to *teach* the Word, is the sum of all wisdom, the heart of all Christian service.
~ Charles E. Fuller

GROW Passages for Week 10

1. Psalm 119:9-16

2. Joshua 1:7-9

3. 1 Peter 2:1-3

4. Proverbs 4:20-22

5. Psalm 145:1-21

Session 11

Fast Facts about Fasting

Matthew 6:16-18

In his book, *Food and Faith in Christian Culture*, Ken Albala writes, "On a chilly morning in March 1522, in the city of Zurich, the printer Christoph Froschauer sat down with his workers and shared a plate of sausages, in open defiance of the Roman Catholic Church, which forbade the consumption of meat during Lent. Froschauer and his men were dragged before the civil magistrates, where he entered his official plea of not guilty on the grounds that he had a heavy load of printing jobs waiting and his men needed the extra sustenance. Such meals were not unheard-of during Lent, and normally for a small fee one could purchase a "dispensation" on the grounds of infirmity, age, or even unusually difficult work. But the printer had never obtained his dispensation and was duly charged.

The city rose in protest, street fighting broke out, and, on April 16, the local prelate Ulrich Zwingli preached a sermon defending the printer's actions not on the grounds of necessity but on the basis of scriptural authority. The New Testament, Zwingli pointed out, nowhere mentions food prohibitions of any kind, all of which were merely invented haphazardly by the Church and could in no way constrain the conscience of men. Neither should there be specific times set aside for fasting: 'as far as time is concerned, the need and use of all food are free, so that whatever food our daily necessity requires, we may use at all times and on all days'. Thus began the Swiss Reformation over a plate of sausages."

Fasting is a discipline not practiced by a wide-ranging mass of Christians, but for Christians to find their full voice before God, fasting is an essential. The purpose for fasting is varied but primarily used as a discipline of self-control and a means to express utter dependence on God. J.I. Packer explains fasting clearly as he writes, "In Scripture we see several purposes for fasting. It's part of the discipline of self-control; it's a way of sharing that we depend on God alone and draw all our strength and resources from him; it's a way of focusing totally on him when seeking his guidance and help, and of showing that you really are in earnest in your quest; it's also, at times, an expression of sorrow and deep repentance, something that a person or community will do in order to acknowledge failure before God and seek his mercy. We tend to think of fasting as going without food. But we can fast from anything. If we love music and decide to miss a concert in order to spend time with God, that is fasting. It is helpful to think of the parallel of human friendship. When friends need to be together, they will cancel all other activities in order to make that possible. There's nothing magical about fasting. It's just one way of telling God that your priority at that moment is to be alone with him, sorting out whatever is necessary, and you have cancelled the meal, party, concert, or whatever else you had planned to do in order to fulfill that priority.

Connecting to the Story

In getting serious about your spiritual life, what is something you need to start doing?

👣 Diving into the Story

What's It All About
The Sermon on the Mount is the first of Jesus' discourses recorded in the Gospels; it combines prophecy to be fulfilled with moral and ethical principles involved in the Kingdom. Jesus focuses on the inner righteousness of the believer rather than the outward show characteristic of the Pharisees. Jesus instructed the disciples that when they gave a gift to the poor, they should not announce it to receive their reward from other people but rather from the Father who sees what they have done and will reward them.

Likewise, there is a right and wrong way to pray. Our prayers should not be a matter of public ostentation, such as standing on street corners so that people will see us praying, rather, we are to pray in secret and be specific with our requests, not babbling vainly like pagans. It was customary for the Pharisees to fast and even disfigure themselves so they would look as if they were suffering more than they really were. Jesus exhorted them to disguise the fact that they were fasting by putting oil on their heads and washing their faces so that only their heavenly Father would know that they were fasting, and he would reward them. Again, the emphasis is on inward purity and devotion rather than outward religious form.

The Big Idea
There may be no spiritual discipline with which we struggle more than closet prayer. It is probably also true that there is no spiritual discipline that we completely neglect quite like fasting. You may have fasted for weight loss or medical purposes. But when was the last time you fasted for purely spiritual reasons? Today we will consider what the Bible teaches about the Christian discipline of fasting.

Christ in the Text

Jesus as the master teacher, continues His discourse on the kind of righteousness he expected of his followers. This righteousness surpasses the legalistic religion of the Pharisees and must be lived so as to impact the world.

#1 Do Not Be Like the Hypocrites (Matthew 6:16)

And when you fast, do not look gloomy like the hypocrites, for they disfigure their faces that their fasting may be seen by others. 'Truly, I say to you they have received their reward.

Matthew 6:16

1. What can Christians do sometimes that can come across as fake or hypocritical?

2. According to Jesus, what practices were associated with the hypocrites and their fasting?

#2 Prepare Your Day as Usual (Matthew 6:17)

But when you fast, anoint your head, and wash your face.

Matthew 6:17

1. Which reason for fasting was new to you or stood out the most?

2. Is there a specific purpose or matter you feel God calling you to fast about?

#3 Seek the Father's Reward (Matthew 6:18)

That your fasting may not be seen by others but by your Father who is in secret. And your Father who sees in secret will reward you.
Matthew 6:18

David Platt has offered an acrostic that sums up Matthew 6:16-18. It is simply FAST:

F-focus on God. You're not doing this for others. You're doing this because you want to seek and know and love and worship God more and more in your life.

A-abstain from food. You abstain from food to the extent of which you are physically able.

S-substitute your time. Substitute the time when you would eat with extra time in prayer and extra time in the word.

T-taste and see the Lord is good. The whole point of fasting is to say, God, you're better. You're better than a sandwich or a steak. You're better than whatever you might want to eat. God, more than I want food, I want intimacy with you. God, I want my hunger to cease. I want your kingdom to come on the earth. And so, I just want to encourage you, if you don't have a regular pattern of fasting to get into a regular pattern of fasting because this is basic to what it means to follow Jesus.

1. What resonates with Platt's acrostic?

2. What other forms of fasting have you seen effective to move your focus off things to the heart of God?

👣 Diving Deeper

1. What is the biggest takeaway from this passage?

2. What are some ways you could apply this passage?

   > *Is there a sin to avoid?*
   > *Is there a promise to claim?*
   > *Is there a command to obey?*
   > *Is there an example to follow?*
   > *Is there praise to give?*

3. What challenges you the most when it comes to fasting?

4. What will you apply specifically this week?

5. Who will hold you accountable this week to your response to Question 4?

"The purpose of fasting is to loosen to some degree the ties which bind us to the world or material surroundings as a whole in order that we may concentrate all of our spiritual powers upon the unseen and eternal things."
~ Ole Hallesby

GROW Passages for Week 11

1. Matthew 6:16-19

2. Daniel 9:1-19

3. Acts 13:1-3

4. Esther 4:1-17

5. Isaiah 58:1-9

Session 12

Making Disciples

Matthew 28:16-20

One of the wonderful things about walking on the sand at the beach is leaving your footprints, at least until the tide rolls in. How many children have walked behind the parents and tried to step into their footprints as they followed their mom or dad? Walking in the steps of another is perhaps the most visual understanding of what it means to make disciples. Making disciples is the mission of the church. Jesus commanded it before ascending back to Heaven, Peter ushered in the mission at Pentecost with the empowerment of the Holy Spirit, and Paul explained it when he said, "And the things you have heard in the presence of many witnesses, commit these to faithful people who will be able to teach others also" (2 Timothy 2:2). Nothing moves the church forward like someone intentionally investing the Gospel lived through their life into another (1 Thess. 2:8). The art of disciple making can never be lost to those who follow Christ, for the one who follows Christ genuinely will be a disciple maker. You cannot help sharing and reflecting the One whom you follow.

In her book, *Deeply Loved*, Keri Wyatt writes, "A rabbi's followers, known as his TALMIDIM in Hebrew, went everywhere with him, not just to hang on his every word and learn theology from him. They followed him everywhere so that they could mimic what he did. They didn't just want to know what he knew; they wanted to do what he did, live as he lived. Ann Spangler and Lois Tverberg note:

To follow a rabbi…involved a literal kind of following, in which disciples often traveled with, lived with and imitated their rabbis, learning not only from what they said but from what they did—from their reactions to everyday life as well as from the manner in which they lived…. This approach to teaching is much more like a traditional apprenticeship than a modern classroom. Jesus still says to us today, "Follow me." He never told us to gain a lot of knowledge about him, but rather, to be with him, to remain in him (see John 15), and then, to live as he would in our place—to do what he did." Disciple making does not happen on Sunday morning during a worship service or in a classroom or even in a home group. Disciple making happens in an intense following of another person who is following Jesus; someone who verbally and visually pours Jesus into another person until they replicate their life in Jesus into another person. One becomes two, two becomes four, four becomes eight and before you know it, a movement of thousands and millions are replicating the life and message of Jesus. Disciple making is the church's mission and that means disciple making is your mission.

Connecting to the Story

Have you ever heard of an *elevator pitch*? An elevator pitch is a clear, yet brief commercial about yourself to share with someone in 30 seconds who you are, what you are about, and what motivates you to do what you do.

As followers of Jesus with a calling on our lives to be disciples who make disciples, we each should have an elevator pitch as it pertains to living out our faith.

Exercise: In your own words, what is your faith elevator pitch to describe your relationship with God and His ministry purpose for you?

My faith elevator pitch is that *I get up in the morning to rescue the religious from religion and the lost from lostness to help others experience a personal relationship with God.*

Diving into the Story

What's It All About

In Matthew 28:16-20, Jesus imbued His followers with a simple yet profound commission. It is the inescapable marching order of every Jesus-follower – we are to intentionally go into our world and make more disciples by sharing the Jesus in us with others so that they too can know and walk with God and seek first His kingdom. To live intentionally missional is neither as hard as it sounds nor as easy as some make it out to be – yet it does require understanding the call and embracing the mission.

Question: What does it mean to live intentionally missional?

When Jesus called the disciples to Himself, He was calling them to something greater than themselves and to a cause that was beyond what they could have ever begun to imagine. Yet for each of them, the cost of followship was the same – complete surrender! They each had to deny themselves, take up their cross, and choose to follow Him if they were ever going to accomplish His mission for their lives to be disciples who made disciples.

Vance Havner explained it this way – Salvation is free and the gift of God is eternal life – yet it is not cheap because it cost God His Son and the Son His life – but it is free. However, when we become believers we become disciples, and that will cost everything we have… (we must never forget) that our Lord was after *disciples*, not mere *joiners*.[ix]

Whenever I consider this incredible calling to be more than a joiner, I am reminded of Paul's charge to the Colossian church. He wrote:

He is the one we proclaim, admonishing and teaching everyone with all wisdom so that we might present everyone fully mature in Christ.
Colossians 1:28

Question: *What does it mean to present a person fully mature in Christ?*

To be fully mature in Christ means a person knows God intimately and personally and that they have learned how to distinguish His voice in their life so that they can respond to His leading and participate in His will for them.

To fulfill God's commission of making disciples requires that maturing believers choose to take personal responsibility for others to aid them in becoming intimate with God. Oswald Chambers explained this idea when he penned that the call of every Christian is to be broken bread and poured out wine to other souls until they are able to feed on God for themselves.[x] Meaning, disciple-making requires personal life-to-life investment. It requires a willingness to get one's hands dirty for the sake of the gospel as we willingly stick our hands into the goop of another person's life to influence them for Christ. As such, disciple-making is accepting the call to personally invest my life with God into the life of another soul. It requires interaction, dialogue, accountability, and responsible mentoring.[xi]

The Big Idea
The mandate of the Christian life is the Great Commission – that is, EVERY believer in Jesus has been called to be a disciple who makes disciples.

Christ in the Text
Jesus is the ultimate disciple-maker. He sets the example for making disciples and sends out those he disciples to make more disciples. Under the authority of Jesus Christ, every believer walks in his footsteps, obeys his commands and lives to please him.

#1 - A Disciple is Available to God (28:16)

Now the eleven disciples went to Galilee, to the mountain to which Jesus had directed them.
Matthew 28:16

1. Why was the disciple's availability an indication of their readiness to take on the mission of Christ?

2. How "available" are you to the mission of Christ? What things could hinder you from being fully available with your time, talent and treasure to the mission of Christ?

3. What proofs have you considered that have convinced you to believe in and follow Jesus?

2 – A Disciple has Affection for God (28:17)

When they saw him, they worshipped him; but some doubted.
Matthew 28:17

1. In your estimation, what is worship?

2. What are the elements or actions of worship?

3. What determines whether or not true worship takes place?

3 – A Disciple Abides in God's Authority (28:18)

And Jesus came and said, "All authority in heaven and on earth has been given to me".
Matthew 28:18

1. Read John 15:1-6. Is it possible to live the Christian life independently of the Holy Spirit?

2. Why is the authority of Christ so critical for Christians to combat the forces of evil that oppose God and his people?

4 – A Disciple Lives for God's Agenda (28:19)

Go therefore and make disciples of all nations, baptizing them in the name of the Father, the Son and the Holy Spirit; teaching them to observe all that I have commanded them.
Matthew 28:19-20a

1. What the command given?

2. What is your strategy for making a disciple of Jesus Christ?

3. Why is teaching people to obey Christ's commandments the core of our mission to make disciples?

4. Read 2 Corinthians 5:20. What does it mean that Christians are ambassadors of Christ and ministers of reconciliation?

5 – A Disciple Waits on God's Assurance (28:20)

And, lo, I am with you always, even to the end of the age.
Matthew 28:20b

1. How do we know that Jesus is with us (other than using this verse)?

2. How does this reality change the way you live your life?

3. Re-read John 10:27. What did Jesus mean that His sheep hear His voice and follow?

4. How does a person hear the voice of God?

Diving Deeper

1. What is the biggest takeaway from this passage?

2. What are some ways you could apply this passage?

   Is there a sin to avoid?
   Is there a promise to claim?
   Is there a command to obey?
   Is there an example to follow?
   Is there praise to give?

3. What challenges do you face when it comes to making disciples? How are you working to resolve those challenges?

4. What will you apply specifically this week?

5. Who will hold you accountable this week to your response to Question 4?

"If you're bored, one thing is for sure: you're not following in the footsteps of Christ."
Mark Batterson, *In a Pit with a Lion on a Snowy Day: How to Survive and Thrive When Opportunity Roars*

👣 GROW Passages for Week 12

1. Matthew 28:16-20

2. 2 Timothy 2:1-7

3. Luke 9:18-27

4. Colossians 1:28-29

5. 1 Corinthians 15:58

Resources Cited for ABIDE

[i] Budziszewski, J. *How to Stay Christian in College*. Carol Stream: NavPress, 2004.
[ii] Cited in Mark Johnston's book, *Saving God: Religion After idolatry*. Princeton: Princeton University Press, 2009.
[iii] Stott, John R.W. *The Message of Ephesians*. Leicester: Intervarsity Press, 1979.
[iv] Cited in *The Pastor's Workshop*. www.thepastorsworkshop.com.
[v] Keller, Timothy and Kathy. *God's Wisdom for Navigating Life*. New York: Viking, 2017.
[vi] Boice, James. *John: Volume 4 John 13-17*. Grand Rapids: Baker Books, 1985.
[vii] Batterson, Mark. *A Trip Around the Sun: Turning Your Everyday Life into the Adventure of a Lifetime*. Grand Rapids: Baker Books, 2015.
[viii] Sumner, Robert. *The Wonders of the Work of God*. Biblical Evangelism Press, 1969.
[ix] Vance Havner.
[x] Oswald Chambers, *My Utmost for His Highest*, (Grand Rapids: Discovery House, 1963), September 30.

[xi] Joey Rodgers, *The Lost Commission: Rediscovering the Call to Make Disciples*, (5 Marks Ministries, 2023), 6-7.